WOLF

By Jenna Grodzicki

Minneapolis, Minnesota

Credits

Cover and title page, © critterbiz/Shutterstock; 3, © AB Photography/iStock; 4–5, © RamiroMarquezPhotos/iStock; 6, © Sasa Stock/Shutterstock; 7, © ViktorCap/iStock; 8, © Iftikhar Ahmad Khan/Shutterstock; 9, © Volodymyr Burdiak/Shutterstock; 10–11, © Cloudtail_the_Snow_Leopard/iStock; 13, © Laura Hedien/Shutterstock; 15, © Holly Kuchera/Shutterstock; 16, © Giedriius / Shutterstock; 17, © John Morrison/iStock; 19, © Alexey Osokin/iStock; 20, © hkuchera/iStock; 21, © blickwinkel/Alamy; 22, © Arcady/Shutterstock; 23, © Andyworks/iStock.

Bearport Publishing Company Product Development Team

President: Jen Jenson; Director of Product Development: Spencer Brinker; Managing Editor: Allison Juda; Associate Editor: Naomi Reich; Senior Designer: Colin O'Dea; Associate Designer: Elena Klinkner; Associate Designer: Kayla Eggert; Product Development Specialist: Anita Stasson

Library of Congress Cataloging-in-Publication Data

Names: Grodzicki, Jenna, 1979- author.
Title: Wolf / by Jenna Grodzicki.
Description: Minneapolis, Minnesota : Bearport Publishing Company, [2024]
  | Series: Library of awesome animals | Includes bibliographical
  references and index.
Identifiers: LCCN 2022058256 (print) | LCCN 2022058257 (ebook) | ISBN
  9798885099974 (library binding) | ISBN 9798888221808 (paperback) | ISBN
  9798888223123 (ebook)
Subjects: LCSH: Wolves--Juvenile literature.
Classification: LCC QL737.C22 .G76 2024 (print) | LCC QL737.C22 (ebook) |
  DDC 599.77--dc23/eng/20221206
LC record available at https://lccn.loc.gov/2022058256
LC ebook record available at https://lccn.loc.gov/2022058257

Copyright © 2024 Bearport Publishing Company. All rights reserved. No part of this publication may be reproduced in whole or in part, stored in any retrieval system, or transmitted in any form or by any means, electronic, mechanical, photocopying, recording, or otherwise, without written permission from the publisher.

For more information, write to Bearport Publishing, 5357 Penn Avenue South, Minneapolis, MN 55419.

Contents

Awesome Wolves! 4
Big Dog 6
There's No Place Like Home 8
Pack Life 10
Howl, Growl, Bark! 12
Time for Dinner 14
Save the Wolves! 16
Puppy Love 18
Growing Up 20

Information Station 22
Glossary 23
Index 24
Read More 24
Learn More Online 24
About the Author 24

AWESOME Wolves!

AWOOOO! A wolf howls as it hunts for dinner. With their sharp teeth and bushy tails, wolves are awesome!

Big Dog

The wolf is the largest member of the dog family. But don't confuse this furry animal with your pet pooch. Unlike **domesticated** dogs, wolves have longer **snouts**. Their strong jaws can crush the bones of their **prey**. And they have long legs that allow them to run nearly 40 miles per hour (65 kph).

A golden retriever

There's No Place Like Home

Most wolves have gray fur, but they can also be black, white, brown, or red depending on where they live. Wolves in the snowy arctic have white fur, while those that make their homes in grasslands, forests, or deserts are darker. These furry animals can be found in these different **habitats** across North America, Europe, Asia, and Africa.

THE RED WOLF IS A TYPE OF WOLF THAT CAN BE FOUND ONLY IN NORTH CAROLINA.

Pack Life

No matter where they make their homes, most wolves live in groups called packs. A pack is usually made up of a mother, a father, and their **offspring**. Sometimes, a wolf that is not related may join, too. The pack members work together to find food, protect their **territory**, and take care of their young.

THERE ARE USUALLY BETWEEN 6 AND 10 WOLVES IN A PACK.

Howl, Growl, Bark!

Since packs work together so closely, their members need a way to **communicate**. Wolves are famous for their howls. This sound might mean a wolf is trying to find others in its pack or letting them know it has spotted something for dinner. But wolves communicate using other sounds, too. Just like their dog relatives, they may growl, bark, yelp, or whine. *GRRRR!*

A WOLF'S HOWL CAN BE HEARD UP TO 10 MILES (16 KM) AWAY.

Time for Dinner

When these predators go hunting, watch out! A wolf pack works together to take down prey. This teamwork allows them to kill animals that are much bigger than they are. The menu includes deer, moose, bison, caribou, and elk. *YUM!* Sometimes, wolves will catch and eat smaller animals, such as rabbits, squirrels, and mice.

WOLVES OFTEN TRAVEL ABOUT 30 MILES (50 KM) A DAY WHEN HUNTING FOR FOOD.

Save the Wolves!

Despite being top predators, some wolves were nearly hunted to **extinction**. Farmers killed them to protect their livestock. Other people killed wolves because they thought they were a **threat** to humans. Today, there are laws to keep wolves safe. There are also places, such as Yellowstone National Park, where people work to help wolf packs grow.

EVEN WITH PROTECTIONS IN PLACE, RED WOLVES AND ETHIOPIAN WOLVES ARE ENDANGERED.

An Ethiopian wolf

Wolves in Yellowstone National Park

Puppy Love

Once a year, wolves **mate**. About two months later, the mother wolf gives birth in a den. She can have up to six babies at a time. The young wolves, called pups, can't see or hear yet. They stay safe inside the den. When they are two weeks old, the pups open their eyes and start to walk.

A GROUP OF WOLF PUPS BORN AT THE SAME TIME IS CALLED A LITTER.

Growing Up

At first, the pups drink milk from their mother's body. But by the time they are six weeks old, the little ones can start eating meat. Soon, they learn how to hunt. At the age of two, the wolves are fully grown and ready to help hunt with the rest of their pack.

WOLVES IN THE WILD LIVE FOR ABOUT EIGHT YEARS.

21

Information Station

WOLVES ARE AWESOME!
LET'S LEARN EVEN MORE ABOUT THEM.

Kind of animal: Wolves are mammals. Most mammals give birth to live young and drink milk from their mothers as babies.

More dogs: In addition to wolves, members of the dog family include coyotes, foxes, jackals, and domesticated dogs.

Size: Wolves can grow to be 7 feet (2 m) long from snout to tail, and about 32 inches (81 cm) tall. That's about the same size as a sofa.

WOLVES AROUND THE WORLD

WHERE WOLVES LIVE

Glossary

communicate to share thoughts, ideas, or information

domesticated tamed to the point where an animal can live with people

endangered being in danger of dying out completely

extinction when an animal dies out completely

habitats places in nature where animals are normally found

mate to come together to have young

offspring an animal's young

predators animals that hunt and eat other animals for food

prey animals that are eaten by other animals

snouts the long, front parts of some animals' heads that includes the nose and usually the jaws and mouth

territory an area of land that belongs to and is defended by a group of animals

threat something that might cause harm

Index

den 18
domesticated 6, 22
Ethiopian wolf 16
fur 6, 8
gray wolf 7
howls 4, 12
hunt 4, 14, 16, 20

mate 18
packs 10, 12, 14, 16, 20
prey 6, 14
pups 18, 20
red wolf 8, 16
teeth 4–5

Read More

Cooke, Tim. *Return to Yellowstone: Gray Wolf Comeback (Saving Animals from the Brink).* Minneapolis: Bearport Publishing Company, 2022.

Humphrey, Natalie. *Wolves in the Wild (Canines in the Wild).* New York: Gareth Stevens Publishing, 2023.

Learn More Online

1. Go to **www.factsurfer.com** or scan the QR code below.
2. Enter "**Wolf**" into the search box.
3. Click on the cover of this book to see a list of websites.

About the Author

Jenna Grodzicki lives on beautiful Cape Cod with her husband and two children. She is both a library media specialist and a writer. She loves to read and go to the beach.